INDIRA
GANDHI
POLITICAL LEADER IN INDIA

SPECIAL LIVES IN HISTORY THAT BECOME

Signature LIVES

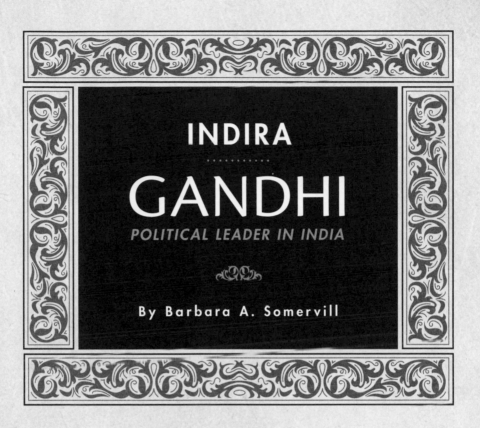

INDIRA
GANDHI
POLITICAL LEADER IN INDIA

By Barbara A. Somervill

Content Adviser: Pradyumna P. Karan, Ph.D.,
Professor of Geography,
University of Kentucky

Reading Adviser: Katie Van Sluys, Ph.D.,
School of Education,
DePaul University

Compass Point Books ◈ Minneapolis, Minnesota

Compass Point Books
3109 West 50th Street, #115
Minneapolis, MN 55410

Visit Compass Point Books on the Internet at *www.compasspointbooks.com*
or e-mail your request to *custserv@compasspointbooks.com*

Managing Editor: Catherine Neitge
Page Production: Blue Tricycle
Photo Researcher: Svetlana Zhurkin
Cartographer: XNR Productions, Inc.
Library Consultant: Kathleen Baxter

Art Director: Jaime Martens
Creative Director: Keith Griffin
Editorial Director: Carol Jones

Library of Congress Cataloging-in-Publication Data
Somervill, Barbara A.
   Indira Gandhi : political leader in India / by Barbara A. Somervill.
      p. cm.—(Signature lives)
   Includes bibliographical references and index.
   ISBN-13: 978-0-7565-1885-1 (library binding)
   ISBN-10: 0-7565-1885-7 (library binding)
   ISBN-13: 978-0-7565-2207-0 (paperback)
   ISBN-10: 0-7565-2207-2 (paperback)
   1. Gandhi, Indira, 1917–1984—Juvenile literature. 2. Prime ministers—
India—Biography—Juvenile literature. I. Title. II. Series.
   DS481.G23S66 2006
   954.04'5092—dc22   [B]   2006027073

Signature Lives

MODERN WORLD

From 1900 to the present day, humanity and the world have undergone major changes. New political ideas resulted in worldwide wars. Fascism and communism divided some countries, and democracy brought others together. Drastic shifts in theories and practice tested the standards of personal freedoms and religious conventions as well as science, technology, and industry. These changes have created a need for world policies and an understanding of international relations. The new mind-set of the modern world includes a focus on humanitarianism and the belief that a global economy has made the world a more connected place.

Table of Contents

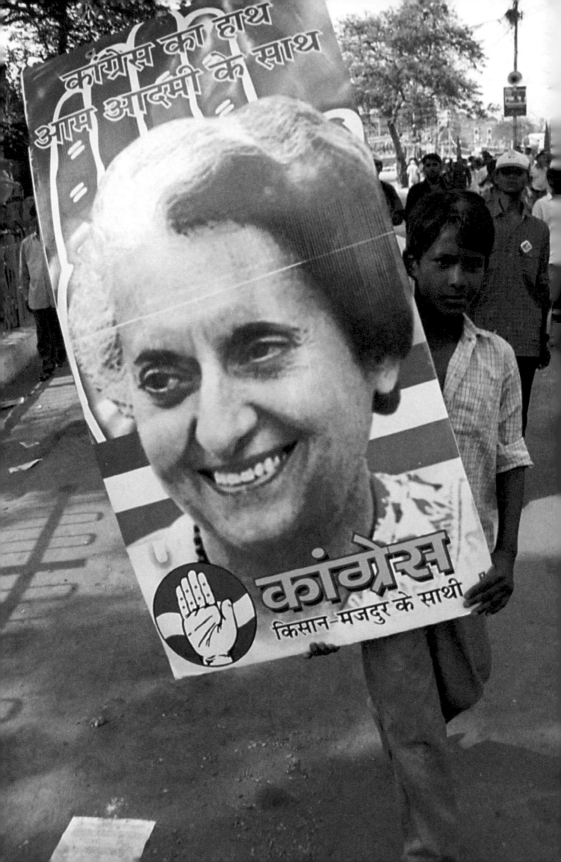

1 A State of Emergency

∽⟨✕⟩∾

In early January 1975, a bomb exploded at a railway station in northeastern India. It wasn't an outside terrorist plot but a political protest by India's own rebel faction. One of Prime Minister Indira Gandhi's Cabinet members, Lalit Narayan Mishra, lay dying. Gandhi accused the rebels of murder, but her political enemies turned the tables and accused her of arranging the assassination. Gandhi seethed, "When I am murdered, they will say I arranged it for myself."

These were troubled times in the southern Asian country of India. Drought left crops withering in the fields and people with empty stomachs. Labor unions went on strike, despite government efforts to force the union members back to work. Rival politicians nipped at Indira Gandhi's popularity.

An image of Indira Gandhi, India's former prime minister, is still used today to rally citizens to vote for the Congress Party.

India is the world's largest democracy and has been an independent nation since 1947. Before that, Great Britain ruled the country as a colonial territory. Today India's population tops 1 billion and ranks second only to China's. Its economy is growing more than 8 percent per year, and the country is modernizing rapidly. The largest cities include its capital, New Delhi, Mumbai (officially changed from Bombay in 1995), and Kolkata (known as Calcutta until 2001). Mumbai's port handles half of India's trade. It is the center of the global outsourcing boom and is the hub of India's music and film industries.

In India, the leader of the party in power serves as prime minister. Loss of popularity turns into loss of votes and, eventually, loss of the prime minister's job. Gandhi's rival for leadership in her own party, the Congress Party, accused her of putting off elections because she feared losing her position as prime minister.

As spring turned into a hot, dry summer, Gandhi suffered one of the worst days of her political career. On election day, June 12, 1975, she experienced three events that created a political explosion and changed the face of Indian politics.

In the morning, Gandhi heard that one of her longtime friends and principal advisers, D.P. Dhar, had died of a heart attack. Still reeling from that news, she was dismayed to find out that the Janata Party had defeated Gandhi's Congress Party in Gujarat, India's westernmost state. This gave the Janata Party, her strongest opposition in Indian politics, more power and placed Gandhi's position on shaky ground.

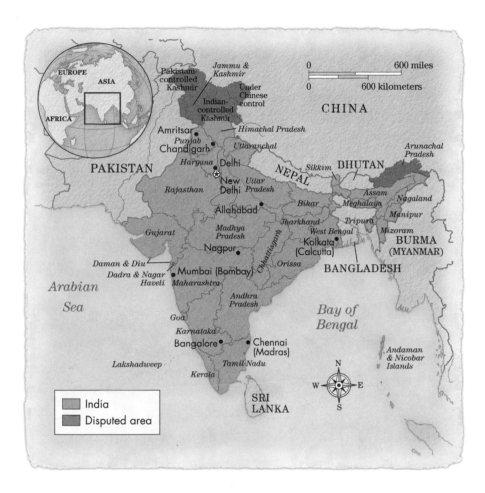

The evening brought even more bad news. The High Court in Allahabad, India, ruled against Gandhi in a nearly four-year-old election dispute. She was found guilty of dishonest election practices, which included using government-paid workers to set up stages and loudspeakers for political speeches. This was a minor offense, but it was taken very seriously. The court declared Gandhi's 1971 parliamentary

India is a little more than one-third the size of the United States and is second only to China in population.

Indira Gandhi's son Sanjay sat in front of paintings of his mother and Mohandas Gandhi, a leader of India's independence movement. The two Gandhi families are not related.

election results invalid. She would lose her seat in the government and her position as prime minister.

Gandhi considered resigning. Her friends and son Sanjay disagreed. Sanjay arranged pro-Indira rallies in the main cities. Crowds chanted *"Indira Zindabad,"* or "Long live Indira." Gandhi appealed to the Indian Supreme Court and received a less-than-acceptable answer. A justice stated that Gandhi could stay in office but could not vote in Parliament. This left her powerless.

"Some drastic, emergent action is needed," said Gandhi. India needed a shake-up, and Gandhi's allies found a way in Article 352 of the Indian Constitution. That article allowed the government to impose a state of emergency when India faced a serious threat. They believed that Gandhi's loss of power was indeed a serious threat to India.

Gandhi and her advisers went directly to India's president, Fakhruddin Ali Ahmed. They wanted the president to declare a state of emergency, giving Gandhi full control of the country. The president wanted to know whether the Cabinet had approved the idea, but Gandhi had avoided discussing the action with her Cabinet ministers. She told the president, "I would have liked to have taken this to the Cabinet, but unfortunately this is not possible tonight. ... I shall mention the matter to the Cabinet first thing tomorrow morning."

The Emergency Order Proc-

India's government system is similar to the British and U.S. governments. The Sansad, or Parliament, is made up of two legislative houses. The upper house, which is like the U.S. Senate, is the Rajya Sabha, or Council of States, with 250 members. The lower house, which is like the U.S. House of Representatives, is the Lok Sabha with 545 members. India's chief of state is the president, elected by members of Parliament and state government legislatures. The real leader is the head of government, the prime minister, who leads the political party with the most seats in Parliament.

lamation was typed and signed by the president. While that happened, Sanjay made a list of his mother's political enemies to be thrown in jail. In the middle of the night, several hundred arrests were made. The Delhi newspapers could not print the story of the state of emergency. Sanjay had arranged for electric power to be cut to districts where newspaper presses were located.

In the morning, the Cabinet met and learned of Indira Gandhi's actions. Even her closest supporters were shocked that Gandhi had arrested her enemies and stifled the news media. They said nothing, however, fearful of landing in jail themselves.

Krishna Menon, an expert on the Indian constitution, dared to speak out against the state of emergency: "It was unconstitutional. That is the worst thing that could have been done. Even for the President to exercise his emergency powers would have been more constitutional."

Gandhi went on radio to address the nation. She tried to reduce public alarm, explaining, "This is nothing to panic about. … [A] deep and widespread conspiracy [had] been brewing ever since I began to

introduce certain progressive measures of benefit to the common man and woman of India." In an effort to preserve democracy, Gandhi basically wiped out all aspects of democratic government. She became a dictator, controlling every aspect of the Indian government.

In July, India's Parliament approved the state of emergency. The lower house, the Lok Sabha, voted 336-39 in favor of the action. The upper house, the

Rajya Sabha, passed the bill 136-33. New amendments were added to the constitution to give Indira Gandhi sweeping powers. Freedom of speech, the press, and assembly, which were guaranteed in the constitution, were temporarily put on hold.

Newspapers and radio broadcasts were censored. No one could openly criticize Prime Minister Gandhi. More than 1,000 political enemies were jailed. Members of Gandhi's own party, the Congress Party, grew increasingly uneasy. That unease grew when Gandhi banned 26 anti-Congress Party political groups.

On the positive side, India had a peaceful period during the 21-month state of emergency. There were no strikes, marches, or riots. Government employees, usually noted for laziness, began showing up for work on time and did their jobs. Crime rates fell. Buses and trains ran on schedule for the first time in memory.

But discontent rippled through India. No matter how much better the average person's life seemed, freedom had disappeared. People who voiced any disapproval of Gandhi wound up in jail cells with other disgruntled Indians.

In August 1975, Sheikh Mujibur Rahman, the president of nearby Bangladesh and one of its founders, was assassinated in his home. The murderers also killed his wife and young children. Hearing of the assassination, Gandhi feared for her family. She panicked, knowing that dictators were

Indira Gandhi spoke to a large crowd of New Delhi students as she led her country through disturbing times.

popular targets for assassins' bullets. Her household became security-conscious for the first time. Indira, her two sons, and their families were heavily guarded in public and at home. No one in her family took a step without a bodyguard by his or her side. Despite her fears, Gandhi could not—and would not—give up her power.

For Indira Gandhi, leadership and power had been part of her birthright. She had been raised as a political princess. Her destiny was to lead India. Yet few people, herself included, realized what path she would follow to fulfill that destiny. 🕭

2 A PAMPERED CHILDHOOD

ᘛᘓ᯽ᘔᘝ

On November 19, 1917, Kamala Kaul Nehru delivered her first and only child. The baby was born at home in the Nehru family compound, called Anand Bhawan, in Allahabad, India. Everyone expected the child of Kamala and Jawaharlal Nehru to be a boy. Sons had great value in traditional Indian families, and daughters did not.

The child's grandmother, Swarup Rani Nehru, announced the baby's birth to waiting family members. She "had not said a son is born but 'it' has been born. In the traditional way she could not bring herself to announce the birth of a daughter," recalled the child's aunt, Vijaya Lakshmi "Nan" Pandit.

Swarup Rani grumbled about the child's sex, but her husband, Motilal, disagreed. The Nehrus were far more Western in their thinking than most Indians. Swarup Rani and Motilal had raised their son, Jawaharlal, and two daughters with equal love and pride. The newborn, "for all we know, may prove better than a thousand sons," said Motilal.

Since ancient times, Hindus believed that people were born into strictly organized castes, or communities. The highest, or aristocratic, caste was Brahmin, the priests. The Kshatryias were soldiers or warriors. The Vaishyas were landowners and merchants. Shudras were artisans and servants. A person was born into a caste and married within that group. No one moved from one caste to another. Below the four castes were the untouchables, or outcasts. Although the caste system was officially abolished in the last century, it still exists unofficially.

The baby girl was named Indira after her great-grandmother Indrani. Jawaharlal added a middle name, Priyadarshini, which means "beautiful to behold." Indira, called Indu by the family, thrived under the constant attention of her parents, grandparents, aunts, and uncles at Anand Bhawan.

Indira grew up in a wealthy, aristocratic family and was treated like a royal princess. The Nehrus belonged to the Brahmin caste, the highest among India's Hindu population. Motilal was head of the household, a position of great power in the family. He was also a political leader and lawyer in Allahabad, a large city in the state of Uttar Pradesh, where the Nehrus lived.

In the early 1900s, India was an odd blend of cultures. Muslim mosques stood alongside Hindu temples and Sikh *gurudwaras*. Women in saris served British tea to guests dressed in Parisian fashions. Wealthy Indian children went to British-run schools and learned how to become perfect British citizens. As young adults, they went to England to attend Oxford or Cambridge universities to finish their education. They returned to India with a deep loyalty to England.

Swarup Rani always dressed in traditional Indian clothing while her husband, Motilal, and young son, Jawaharlal, wore British styles.

In Allahabad, few Indians loved all things British more than Motilal Nehru. Following Motilal's lead, most of the Nehru family dressed in Western clothes and honored British rule. Motilal spoiled Indu, who, in turn, adored and respected her grandfather. He left her with a sense of Indian pride and a touch of wisdom. Later in life, she recalled:

> *My grandfather once told me that there are two kinds of people: those who work and those who take the credit. He told me to try to be in the first group; there was less competition there.*

Despite his Western dress and furnishings, there were some areas in which Motilal followed his Indian heritage. Marriage, for example, was not a matter of choice but an arrangement between two families. Motilal arranged just such a marriage for Indira's father. The marriage did not have a major impact on Jawaharlal's life. He brought his new bride, Kamala Kaul, to live at Anand Bhawan, and later in life Jawaharlal recalled:

> *She had no formal education; her mind had not gone through the educational process ... Essentially she was an Indian girl, and, more particularly, a Kashmiri girl—sensitive and proud, childlike and grown-up, foolish and wise.*

Early in the marriage, Jawaharlal simply did not love Kamala and, for the most part, ignored her. The Nehru women did not ignore Kamala, however. They found her an easy target for taunting and abuse, which led to Kamala's spending most of her time in her rooms. As a young child, Indu spent hours alone

Jawaharal and Kamala Nehru on their wedding day, February 8, 1916

with her mother, listening to stories and learning the Hindi language. The two formed a close bond that influenced Indira throughout her life.

Indira was always treated like the family princess, spoiled and indulged in every way. But she saw the way her mother was treated. Indira decided early in life that she would never allow anyone to treat her so badly. She kept this promise.

When Indira was a toddler, the relationship between the British rulers and the Indian subjects began to change. The event that sparked a fire of rebellion occurred on April 13, 1919, in the holy city of Amritsar in the northern state of Punjab. On that day, 20,000 unarmed people were gathered in a park to attend a protest meeting and to celebrate the Hindu New Year. Britain's General Reginald Dyer led 150 soldiers to the park to force the Indians to leave. With no word of warning, the soldiers fired on the crowd, leaving 379 dead and 1,200 badly wounded. The event enraged Indians against British rule and encouraged the fight for independence. Suddenly, the political atmosphere changed, and the Nehru family's love of all things British changed, too.

Indira's family stepped into politics with zeal, and, young as she was, Indira was exposed to the most important people in 20th-century India. When she was about 5, she met Mohandas Gandhi, a beloved political leader who fought for India's independence

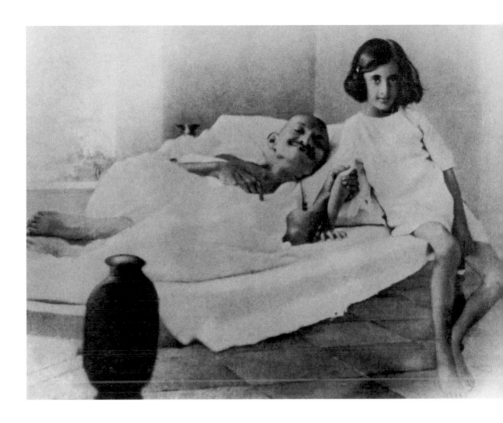

Indira at age 6 with Mohandas Gandhi, who was weak from fasting in his quest for Hindu-Muslim unity

from Great Britain. Although not related to him, she looked on Gandhi as an uncle who gave good advice. Gandhi was to Indu "an elder in the family to whom I went with difficulties and problems which he treated with the grave seriousness which was due to the large-eyed and solemn child I was."

Mohandas Gandhi urged Indians to follow a path of civil disobedience. He led nonviolent protests against British laws and taxes. He asked his followers to boycott British goods, schools, books, and clothing. Indira's family quickly committed to anti-British life.

Mohandas K. Gandhi (1869–1948), called Mahatma, or "Great Soul," brought a sense of nationwide purpose to India under British rule. He inspired Indians to rebel against the British and urged nonviolent protests against the government. He encouraged Indians to boycott all things British, including paying taxes and attending British-run schools. His story is one of courage, determination, and religious will. Even those who disagreed with Gandhi admired and respected him. Gandhi's followers revered their leader for his dedication to Indian independence.

They burned their English clothes in a symbolic bonfire. The Nehru men spoke out against unfair British taxes and ended up in jail.

Indian women quickly joined the protests. They tended Indians wounded in protests by the police. They hid rebels in their homes. They too ended up in jail. And so young Indira spent many afternoons making jailhouse visits to her father, grandfather, aunts, and cousins. Kamala also found a way to support her husband—she became an avid Gandhi follower. As an adult, Indira recalled:

Many people knew the part which was played by my grandfather and my father. But, in my opinion, a more important part was played by my mother. When my father wanted to join Gandhiji and to change the whole way of life … the whole family was against it. It was only my mother's courageous and persistent support and encouragement that enabled him to take this step which made such a difference not only to our family but the history of modern India.

While Jawaharlal sat in jail for a few months, Kamala worried that Indira was not getting the education she needed. Jawaharlal asked his father, now released from prison, to arrange for some formal schooling for Indu. At first, Indu attended the Allahabad Modern School, which offered a low-quality, Indian education. Motilal decided to send Indu to St. Cecilia's, a small school run by three English women with the last name of Cameron. Jawaharlal exploded. St. Cecilia's fell under the Gandhi boycott. In addition, Jawaharlal worried that his Indian daughter would become a British-style little girl under the Camerons' teaching. He needn't

Indira's family in 1927: (standing, from left) her father, Jawaharlal, her aunt, Vijaya Lakshmi Pandit, her aunt, Krishna Nehru, Indira, and her uncle, Ranjit Pandit; (seated, from left) her grandmother, Swarup Rani, her grandfather, Motilal, and her mother, Kamala

have worried. Indira felt out of place at St. Cecilia's. She said, "All the other girls wore—well, other kinds of clothes. I had to wear *khadi*, homespun cloth. It was very rough and stiff, and very uncomfortable."

An argument developed between father and son, and Mohandas Gandhi was asked to step in. Gandhi stated flatly that St. Cecilia's did indeed come under the boycott. St. Cecilia's was out, and private tutors arrived at Anand Bhawan to teach Indira.

While at home, Indira witnessed violence first-hand just beyond the family compound. One evening, she looked out a window and saw a policeman chasing someone. The man was an Indian patriot named Chandrasekhar Azad. Supposedly this man had plotted the murder of a local British official. The police surrounded Azad and shot him. Indira said, "I saw the flashes and heard the shots. Violence is terrifying, you know. I saw all this from the house, and I felt numb, as though I had been dropped in very hot water or very cold water."

School and violent events became less important when a family crisis occurred. In 1926, Kamala Nehru was very ill with tuberculosis, an often deadly lung disease. Her doctors advised going to a Swiss sanatorium for her health. The Nehrus began an adventure that Indira would remember all her life. They traveled by ship through the Suez Canal. Jawaharlal taught Indira about Egypt and its rich

*Indira, 13,
with her father
and mother*

history. The family went to Venice, then into the Alps and Switzerland. While Kamala regained her health, Indira went to L'Ecole Nouvelle (the New School) in Bex, Switzerland. Indira studied French there and learned how to ski.

This was a marvelous time for Indira. It was the first time her family had been together without all the Nehru relatives. Kamala, though sick, blossomed under the attention of Jawaharlal and Indira. And because Kamala recovered, the time in Switzerland seemed more like a family vacation than the hospital visit that it was. ॐ

3 EUROPE, FEROZE, AND MARRIAGE

Within a year, the family returned to India, and Indira was enrolled in St. Mary's School. Although the school was British in nature, Jawaharlal did not object to it because it provided a good education. At home, Indira studied Hindi and Indian history with her mother.

Shortly after he arrived home, Jawaharlal joined Motilal at a meeting of the Indian National Congress in Madras, a city in southeastern India. Motilal led the meeting, which ended up in a serious clash between father and son. Motilal and his followers believed in tradition and wanted to remain connected to Great Britain. For Jawaharlal and his friends, only complete independence would do.

Two years later, Congress met again in Lahore,

Mohandas Gandhi and his followers protested India's salt tax by refusing to pay it and walking 240 miles (384 kilometers) to the sea.

31

which today is a city in Pakistan. During the years, the independence movement had grown, and Motilal realized that his views no longer represented the majority opinion. Leadership passed from Motilal to his son.

On January 26, 1930, Indira watched with pride as her father spoke to the public. She saw thousands of Indians pledge to fight for independence. Over the weeks to come, Indian prisons filled with Indian protesters. Women left the safety of their homes to support the cause. In the Nehru family, both men and women joined the protests. Luckily, Indira knew the route to the local jail by heart and could visit her imprisoned family members on a regular basis.

Mohandas Gandhi called for a protest against the salt tax—the salt *satyagraha*. Gandhi himself coined the word to define the philosophy of nonviolent resistance used in India's struggle for independence. In his act of civil disobedience, Gandhi refused to pay the salt tax. Instead, he walked 240 miles (384 kilometers) to the seashore and collected salt for free.

Indira ached to become part of the independence movement. She, too, wanted to join the Congress Party and take the pledge to fight for independence, but her parents told her she was much too young. Instead, she organized what she called the Monkey Brigade. The children's group put up posters, addressed envelopes, delivered messages, and ran other errands. It was all she could do at 12 years old.

Again her father spent time in prison. This time, however, he decided to further Indira's learning through a series of letters. These letters between father and daughter would span several decades. The two exchanged daily thoughts, experiences, and emotions. The distance between them was never so great that a postage stamp couldn't bridge the gap.

During the next few years, Nehru became a frequent prison resident. When not in prison, he and his family traveled throughout India encouraging people to stand up against British rule.

Indian children listened to many legends and tales, including the Ramayana stories. These stories tell about the exploits of Lord Rama, the ideal man and king. In one tale, Lord Rama prepared to invade the kingdom of Lanka and free his captured wife, Sita. He had no soldiers to help, so he called on an army of monkeys and bears to help him. It was this Monkey Brigade that Indira Gandhi referred to as a child.

In 1934, the Nehrus traveled through West Bengal in northeastern India. They visited Visva-Bharati, a school founded by the great Indian writer and poet Rabindranath Tagore. The unconventional school blended methods of learning from the East and West. Finally they had found a school that could teach Indira what she needed to learn, yet could ensure she retained a sense of Indian identity.

Jawaharlal needn't have worried about Indira's

education. She was a natural learner and an avid reader. She read biographies and political histories of independence movements and rebellions, themes close to her heart. Books filled her empty hours and expanded her understanding of the world. Indira felt quite comfortable in the educational environment encouraged by Tagore.

Writer, teacher, and philosopher Rabindranath Tagore won the Nobel Prize for literature in 1913.

Bad news came within a year after Indira began studying at Tagore's school. Tuberculosis struck Kamala again, and she needed to return to Switzerland. Since Jawaharlal was back in prison, Indira accompanied her mother there.

A family friend, Feroze Gandhi, helped care for Kamala in Switzerland. He had visited Anand Bhawan many times and was a familiar face. Feroze was short and solid, with pale skin and dark eyes and hair. While not related to Mohandas Gandhi, Feroze actively supported radical causes, and Indian independence was high on his list. His family disagreed, and Feroze got in trouble at home for his contact with the independence-minded Nehrus.

Jawaharlal was eventually released from prison to go to Switzerland and join his wife. Indira and her father were by Kamala's side when she died in February 1936 at the age of 36. After she died, Jawaharlal needed to return to India and the independence movement. He wanted Indira to continue her education, and she agreed, as long as she could go to school in England. There was a reason behind her choice: Feroze Gandhi attended the London School of Economics. "I considered him more as a friend; it was a link with the family and India," Indira said.

Indira and her father on their way to England where she would attend school

Indira attended the Badminton School in Bristol,

a posh English private school. Among her classmates was Iris Murdoch, who later became a popular novelist. To Iris, Indira seemed "intensely worried about her father and her country and thoroughly uncertain about the future." Indira appeared shy, retiring, and distant to her English friends.

From Badminton, Indira went to Somerville College at Oxford University. She saw Feroze on weekends and holidays. Together they pursued an interest in Labour Party politics and socialism. They belonged to the Left Book Club, a group promoting socialist literature.

Indira did well in the subjects she liked—history, political science, and economics. Her downfall was

Indira (third from left in fourth row) and other first-year students at Somerville College, Oxford University

Latin. Every Oxford student had to study and pass a Latin exam. After two tries and two failures, Indira had to leave Oxford. She decided to return to India.

However, it was 1941, and the world was at war. Indira's trip from England to India was made longer because the ship had to dodge German submarines and could not pass through the Suez Canal because of the hostilities in the Mediterranean Sea. Feroze traveled with Indira, and the two were in love.

The ship put into port at Durban, South Africa, and local Indian merchants hosted Indira and Feroze. They arranged a tour of the city, which was supposed to entertain the lovely Miss Nehru. Instead, she became outraged. At a dinner one evening, she spoke out against the injustice of apartheid. She scolded the merchants about their lack of concern for the black people living there. Her visit to South Africa was short, but Indira made quite an impression before she left.

When Indira arrived in Bombay, India, her father was again in prison. She had news, but it would have to wait. Feroze had proposed marriage several times, and Indira had accepted in 1937. Years later, she wrote: "It was the end of summer, and Paris was bathed in sunshine and her heart truly seemed to be young and gay. ... The whole city was full of people who were young and in a holiday mood." She kept her engagement secret for four years.

Indira couldn't tell her father she planned to

Indira did not tell her father about her wedding plans for several years.

marry. Feroze would never be his choice of a husband for her. She knew the problems that lay ahead:

> *Feroze was a Parsi. [A member of a Zoroastrian community that came to India from Persia to escape religious persecution.] In marrying him I was breaking age-old traditions. It was an intercommunity and interreligion marriage. And it did "raise a storm." Yet it was not the first mixed marriage. ... There is no doubt that many people, including my own family, were very upset.*

When Jawaharlal found out about the proposed marriage, he openly opposed it. He had his reasons, not the least of which was his belief that Feroze could not afford to support Indira in the comfort she'd enjoyed all her life. Father and daughter were stubborn. Eventually Indira's will won out, but not before seemingly the entire nation voiced its opinion.

Once he was convinced that Indira was going to marry Feroze no matter what he said, Jawaharlal made a public statement in favor of the marriage:

> *When I was assured that Indira and Feroze wanted to marry one another, I accepted willingly their decision and I told them that it had my blessing. Mahatma Gandhi, whose opinion I value not only in public affairs but in private matters also, gave his blessings to the proposal.*

Mohandas Gandhi wrote an open letter to critics who opposed the marriage. He said, "Feroze Gandhi has been for years an intimate of the Nehru family. He nursed Kamala Nehru in her sickness. He was like a son to her. A natural intimacy grew up between them [Indira and Feroze]."

The wedding took place on March 26, 1942, at Anand Bhawan. Although the couple wanted a small, private affair, Mohandas Gandhi suggested otherwise. He felt that so many people shared an interest—

Ceremonial rites using a fire took place during the wedding of Indira Nehru and Feroze Gandhi.

positive or negative—in the marriage that it should be a public celebration. Garlands of marigolds adorned Anand Bhawan. The Nehru family displayed hundreds of presents sent by friends and relatives.

The groom arrived in an *achkan*, a long coat made of homespun cloth, and tight trousers. He looked happy, excited, and quite handsome. The bride chose a simple sari of pink cotton. The yarn to make the sari had been spun by her father while in prison. Although it was the custom for brides to wear nearly 2 pounds (907 grams) of gold jewelry at their weddings, Indira chose to wear fresh flowers.

The ceremony was neither religious nor civil. In India at the time, few people married outside their religion. Indira and Feroze chose not to reject their own religions, nor would they say they did not follow a religion, which would have made them eligible for a civil wedding. A compromise was needed for the ceremony.

A fire was lit in the center of the wedding area. A Vedic hymn satisfied both Hindus and Parsis. A Hindu priest led the chanting and reading of poetic verses. Indian writer and international journalist Pranay Gupte described what happened next:

> *With the chanting of hymns over, Jawaharlal placed Indira's hand in Feroze's. Together, their hands clasped and with a corner of the bride's sari tied to the bridegroom's achkan, they took seven steps around the fire, binding themselves into the eternal, irrevocable union.*

The couple headed off to Kashmir for their honeymoon. Indira loved the mountains and had enjoyed many family trips to the region as a child. Now she was a woman and a wife. Like many brides, she expected to have a perfect marriage. She didn't realize that politics would invade her marriage as it had her childhood. ℘

4 AN INDEPENDENT INDIA

Chapter

꧂

After their months-long honeymoon, Indira and Feroze could hardly wait to get back to Allahabad and the independence movement. Indira hoped to live in Anand Bhawan with the rest of the Nehrus, but Feroze had a different idea. He was determined that Indira would be a Gandhi, make a home for him, and be a good wife. He had no idea that Indira's sense of duty would make her choose her father's work over her husband's needs.

In August 1942, the All India Congress Committee met in Bombay, where Mahatma Gandhi introduced a new campaign: Quit India. It was a plan to oust Great Britain from India once and for all. Police immediately picked up Mahatma Gandhi, Jawaharlal Nehru, and the other Congress Committee leaders in a predawn raid. Jawaharlal spent his prison time in Ahmadnagar, a 16th-century fortress south of Bombay. This time he spent nearly three years in jail, his longest and last prison sentence.

Freedom fighters protested. They blew up police stations and courthouses, railway lines, and bridges. They cut telegraph and telephone lines to slow communications between British troops. The police reacted by hurling tear gas into crowds and making thousands of arrests.

Feroze and Indira took a stand by joining the resistance. Feroze went underground, and the couple sent messages to each other via workers in the Quit India movement. Indira moved into Anand Bhawan because someone needed to take care of the house while her father was in prison. She viewed the events

Nehru (left), Gandhi, and others planned a campaign of civil disobedience against British rule. They were all jailed.

of the next few months as a kind of game. The police had warrants out to arrest independence leaders, and Indira Gandhi and friends hid those leaders in their homes. Lal Bahadur Shastri, a future prime minister, stayed upstairs in Anand Bhawan while Indira pled ignorance of his whereabouts to the police at the gate. Indira's role as a rebel became common knowledge, and rumors flew that she would be arrested.

> *I sent word to Feroze. He happened to be in Allahabad and felt that there was no point in getting arrested so tamely and that it would be better to organize a meeting at least. … Our meeting was banned. … British soldiers were patrolling all the streets not knowing where it would be. … I came out and addressed the gathering. Soon the military came aiming their guns at us. We were surrounded on all sides, and one chap had his bayonet almost touching me. Feroze, who was watching from upstairs, became very excited. He forgot about being underground and he rushed out and said, "Either you shoot or you get away from here." We were all arrested.*

Indira would spend nine months in Naini prison. The superintendent placed her in a small women's cell that she shared with her aunt Nan Pandit and her cousin Chandralekha, along with a few other Indian protesters. The women divided the space into

Nan Pandit, Indira's aunt, went on to have a long diplomatic career. She was the first female president of the U.N. General Assembly.

personal areas, which provided the only privacy in the jail. They each kept their area spotless and even gave their spaces names. Indira called her area Chimborazo after a favored mountain area.

Indira Gandhi's health began to fail, and a doctor came to examine her. Although he recommended a better diet and other changes, her jailers ignored the recommendations. Indira later said:

Herded together like animals, devoid of dignity of privacy, debarred not only from outside company or news but from all beauty and colour, softness and grace, the ground, the walls, everything around us was mud coloured and so became our jail-washed clothes. Even our food tasted gritty. Through the barred apertures [windows] we were exposed to the loo (hot summer wind) and dust storms, the monsoon downpour and the winter cold.

Indira's release came on May 13, 1943. Feroze,

who had also been imprisoned, got out of jail in August. They returned to Allahabad, where Indira took charge of Anand Bhawan while Feroze took to gardening on the grounds. He turned the gardens into a showplace. At the same time, he began writing freelance magazine articles about his travels in Europe. Indira and Feroze settled into relatively normal married life.

A year later, Indira delivered her first son, Rajiv, at her aunt's home in Bombay. The birth was remarkably easy, and both Indira and Feroze were delighted with their son. Jawaharlal, still in prison, offered possible names for the child through letters. Indira later said:

> *A friend of mine also gave me a list and it included Rajiv. Until then I had never heard of anybody called Rajiv. It means lotus and Kamal, my mother's name [,] also means lotus. My son's real name is Rajiv Ratna. Ratna means the same as Jawahar, so it was a combination of both my parents' names.*

Jawaharlal Nehru did not see his first grandchild until Rajiv was nearly a year old. In 1945, he was finally released from prison. He immediately arranged a job for Feroze with a newspaper he owned in Lucknow. He appointed Feroze as managing editor of *The National Herald*, and the Gandhis moved into a small cottage in Lucknow. Feroze proved quite successful

Mohandas Gandhi visited political prisoners in Calcutta before India's independence.

at running the paper. He was a hardworking, friendly, easygoing man. An editor at the paper remarked: "He was a man with the common touch. He often worked in the press day and night. He loved machines[;] he did not mind the ink and the soot. This endeared him to the workers."

Jawaharlal moved to Delhi, the heart of the soon-to-be-independent Indian government. Now began the tug of war that would tear Indira's marriage apart. Her father worked 16 hours a day getting India ready for independence, and he desperately needed someone to oversee his home, meals, laundry, and personal schedule. That person could only be Indira, but Feroze expected Indira to stay in Lucknow with him. Month after month, she traveled the nearly 300-mile (480 km) journey between the two cities on the train with Rajiv.

In December 1946, Indira gave birth to her second son. She was at her father's home in Delhi when she delivered, and Feroze had come to be with her. Indira named the child Sanjay. The delivery was a difficult one, and Indira almost died. There would be no more children for the Gandhis. As a mother, Indira had good intentions. She said:

> *I was determined to devote full time to my children. A child's need of his mother's love and care is as urgent and fundamental as that of a plant for sunshine and water. To a mother, her children must always come first, because they depend on her in a very special way. ... I did not like the idea of anyone else attending to their needs and I tried to do as much for them as I could.*

Meanwhile, the British had found that fighting against independence was time-consuming and expensive. Between 1940 and 1942, thousands of members of India's Congress were arrested. The prisoners had to be housed, fed, and clothed, and guards paid to work in the prisons. Although the rebellion was passive in the beginning, it demanded tremendous resources from the British. Within India,

The British East India Company, chartered in 1600 by Queen Elizabeth I, initially came to India to buy spices and silk. The company stayed, and by 1756, it controlled the rich Ganges Delta. Soon British rule extended over most of the area. India provided Britain with a secure source of raw materials and a guaranteed market for British goods. Prosperity for the common people did not exist under British rule. This colonial exploitation led to the Indian Mutiny of 1857, and the British East India Company came to an end. For roughly the next century, the British government ruled India with a stern hand.

Congress did not trust the British. The Muslim League, a powerful political group that was also on the rise, did not trust Congress or the British.

After World War II, Great Britain had major concerns at home, including rebuilding the country and paying off war debts. It didn't need more problems in India. In August 1946, rioting and massacres broke out in northern India. In 1947, the British decided to divide India into two nations: India and Pakistan. Independence for India was next.

Independence came at midnight on August 14, 1947. People sang and danced in the streets. Millions of temple bells pealed in every city and town. Bonfires, candles, and torches lit the night. But what would freedom bring? Many hoped they would see an end to oppression.

Jawaharlal Nehru became the first Indian prime minister. One minute before midnight that historic night, Nehru rose to speak in Parliament:

Jawaharlal Nehru, India's first prime minister, spoke to a huge crowd during India's independence celebration on August 15, 1947.

Long years ago we made a tryst with destiny and now the time comes when we shall redeem our pledge, not wholly or in full measure but very substantially. At the stroke of the midnight hour when the world sleeps, India will awake to life and freedom.

Indira was thrilled that victory was finally at hand. She wrote: "It is one of the proudest and most exciting moments in my life. It was the culmination which so many people had fought for. Yet, when

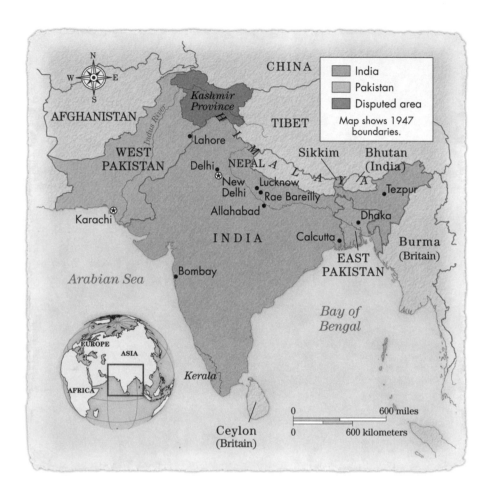

The new country of Pakistan was divided into eastern and western sections with India in between.

it actually came, I think one was more numbed than anything."

Independence brought changes, and not all were welcome. The new country of Pakistan would be a homeland for Muslims. It was made up of Bengali East Pakistan and West Pakistan. The two parts of the new country straddled the western and eastern borders of India and were separated by more than

1,000 miles (1,600 km) of India's land. As communal violence broke out, the Hindus who had remained in Pakistan left for India. In addition, most Muslims had chosen to remain in secular India (which today has the world's second-largest Muslim population after Indonesia).

Tragedy came less than six months after India's independence. Mohandas Gandhi was assassinated in January 1948 by a Hindu fanatic who opposed his peace dealings with Muslims. His death shocked the country. He had been a national hero, an advocate of peace, and a leader for independence.

For the Nehru-Gandhi family, the loss struck deep. Indira had known Mohandas Gandhi since childhood and had visited him the day before he died. He was a family friend and adviser, and she could not imagine what would happen to India without their "Great Soul." She later said, "His spirit was with us and a priceless legacy of faith, courage, and determination to follow the path of duty and of service to the people of India which was so dear to his heart."

Mohandas Gandhi was an English-educated lawyer who is considered the father of India

Indira Gandhi often traveled with her father and served as his first lady.

Indira's importance to her father increased. Despite the demands of being a wife and a mother, she felt obliged to serve as India's first lady. She ran her father's household and ran interference between him and the people who wished to see him. She hosted state dinners, although she found little joy in the endless hours and demands of government service. Indira compared being first lady of India to "walking on a tight rope to adhere close enough to the formal side of protocol so as not to offend even the most particular of dignitaries and yet manage not to stifle the human element and to keep the function interesting and homely."

While Indira dined with world leaders, Ferozc remained in Lucknow, sullen and resentful. To punish Indira and ease his own loneliness, he began dating women. Then in 1952, Feroze stood for election to Parliament in the Rae Bareilly voting district in northern India. He won handily and moved to Delhi to take his seat in the Lok Sabha. He ate dinner at Teen Murti House, the prime minister's residence, but refused to live there. Even dinners became a thorn in his side, since Indira sat among the elite, and Feroze sat among the lowest governmental guests.

For two years, Feroze sat in the Congress and said nothing. Then an idea came to him. He could avenge himself against the Nehrus by embarrassing them in public. He chose to strike through speeches in the Lok Sabha that denounced illegal insurance practices. The targets of these strikes were Jawaharlal Nehru's good friends.

Communism became another sword that divided Indira and Feroze. They both dabbled in communism while in England, and Feroze had stayed in contact with his communist friends. Indira had changed and voiced her disapproval of communism, while Feroze openly supported socialistic programs—tossing another political pie in Jawaharlal's face.

Indira Gandhi with her sons Rajiv (center) and Sanjay in the early 1950s

Feroze earned a reputation as a giant killer among lawmakers. If he thought his actions would bring Indira back to his side, he was mistaken. She felt outraged, betrayed, and depressed about her husband and her marriage.

Still Feroze continued to eat at Teen Murti House. He played with his sons and had them come to stay with him on the weekends. When he was with them, Feroze gave his sons his undivided attention. They built toy trains, ran cars, and played with the household pets. An avid gardener, Feroze taught his sons how to grow roses and native Indian flowers.

Indira spent time with her children as often as she could. She loved children and became a trustee of the Indian Council for Child Welfare. She founded Bal Bhavan, an arts school for underprivileged children, and also Bal Sahyog, a house for homeless children in Delhi.

Her job as first lady required her to travel with her father. They made trips to Russia, the United States, and several European countries, as well as touring throughout India. In 1958, Indira and Jawaharlal Nehru traveled to neighboring Bhutan on horseback, since there were few passable roads into the mountainous country.

While on the trip, Indira got word that Feroze had suffered a heart attack. She returned to Delhi and took over nursing her husband. This led to the longest time they'd spent together in years and was a positive lift to their marriage. It was a reunion that would last only until India's political demands stole Indira away again. ♋

5 THE CONGRESS PRESIDENT

Chapter

❧❧❧

When the prime minister's daughter became the political party president in 1959, many politicians cried "Unfair!" It became a major political issue. They questioned whether Indira was chosen as a favor to her father. Had they talked to Nehru, they would have found that he was not keen on his daughter's serving in a Congress Party leadership position.

During her year as president, she faced the growth of communism in Kerala, India. The Marxist party in that southwest Indian region won the local election. It immediately began an education program that taught Marxism in school, including the speeches of Mao Tse-tung, the Chinese dictator. Indira spoke out strongly against the Kerala government, and her husband, Feroze, spoke out against Indira. The marriage that had been healed by Feroze's heart attack suffered another serious blow. Indira wrote to a friend:

> *A veritable sea of trouble is engulfing me. On the domestic front, Feroze has always resented my very existence, but since I have become President of the Congress party he exudes such hostility that it seems to poison the air.*

Although elected for a two-year term, Indira served only one year. During that time, she managed to wipe out party debt and leave a healthy balance moving forward. She addressed refugee problems, children's health, women's rights, and poverty. She resigned, claiming poor health, although it is likely that stress and marriage problems were the key factors in her decision.

In an interview with *Blitz* newspaper, Nehru said, "It is well known that I did not groom her or help her in any way to become the Congress Party President—but she did; and I am told even by people who do not like me or my policies that she made a very good president."

Although she gave up party leadership, Indira did not give up politics. On September 7, 1960, she was in Kerala dealing with the communist situation when she got word that Feroze had suffered another heart attack. He had been at a session in Parliament when he started having chest pains. He drove himself to Willingdon Nursing Home. By the time Indira arrived, Feroze was nearly gone. He died the following morning.

Indira's guilt over neglecting her husband overwhelmed her. She became sick, drawn, pale, and visibly stressed. She had always thought that when her father finished with politics, she would have the time to repair her marriage. The hope died with Feroze. She later said:

Her husband's death was very hard on Gandhi and she suffered for many years.

> *I was actually physically ill. It upset my whole being for years, which is strange, because after all he was very ill and I should have expected that he would die. However, it was not just a mental shock, but it was as though somebody had cut me in two.*

Feroze's body was returned to Teen Murti House, where Indira personally washed and dressed the

Hindu funeral rites are steeped in tradition. Adults who die are always cremated because it is believed that cremation helps the soul escape from the body. A priest and male family member conduct the rites. Widows or widowers wear white, which is the Indian color of mourning. Often widows shave their heads, sleep on the floor, and eat plain, unspiced foods. Long ago, widows were expected to commit suttee, burning themselves alive on their husbands' funeral pyres. The British outlawed suttee in 1829.

body. Thousands of people showed up for the funeral. Indira's sons, away at school, came home for the ceremony. At the cremation site, Indira wore white, her sorrow written on her face. As tradition demanded, 16-year-old Rajiv lit the funeral pyre.

After Rajiv went back to school, Indira wrote to him:

> *I could not really cry—but now I have begun to cry and don't seem to be able to stop. … This dreadful thing has happened just when I thought everything was going well and that we might all live together as a family again.*

Indira needed to keep busy. Within a few months, she toured Mexico, spoke at several public events in the United States, and stopped in Paris for a United Nations meeting. Still, the feeling of desperation would not leave her. "The fits of dark dark despair and depression do come, but that is something I have always had—but on the whole I have got over that awful self-pity and preoccupation with my own sorrow."

In 1962, border disputes between India and China came to a head, with China attacking in the northeast. Panic raced through the threatened Assam region and the cities of Delhi and Calcutta. People in the border regions begged for help in fleeing the area.

There was little food, and local officials had fled to save their own lives. At the height of the action, and against military advice, Indira went to Tezpur, a city only 30 miles (48 km) from China's army. She wanted to see what she could do to help her people.

Jawaharlal Nehru, who was getting old, faced the Chinese situation without the strength he had shown in the past. He spoke on All-India Radio as though Assam and other regions had already been lost to the Chinese. The conflict ended with China proposing a cease-fire after defeating Indian forces in Aksai Chin, which China still controls today. Nehru continued to decline, and in 1964, he suffered a stroke that left him in a wheelchair. Indira's role as first lady demanded more of her. She virtually ran the country while her father slowly regained his health.

On May 26, Nehru suffered serious pain in his stomach. A doctor was summoned to Teen Murti House, but nothing could be done. Nehru spoke to Indira, saying, "I have finished my work." He died the next day at the age of 74.

Jawaharlal Nehru's body lay in state, covered with lilies, marigolds, and roses. Blocks of ice sat near the body, with fans blowing at full speed to slow the body's decay. Mourners poured through Teen Murti House to view Nehru. The nation wept along with Indira and her sons.

Trevor Drieberg, a Delhi editor, remembered his feelings after hearing of Nehru's death:

> *Nehru is dead, I repeated to myself. I shall never see Nehru again. It seemed unbelievable. Nehru was India. Nehru was universal. He represented all the basic decencies of human life. What now? And I thought of all the rats who were busy right at the moment sharpening their claws and preening their whiskers for the great race that would now begin.*

Rajiv and Sanjay Gandhi carried the ashes of their grandfather Jawaharlal Nehru in a funeral procession from New Delhi to Allahabad.

The cremation was held at Rajghat. Indira stood quietly to the side. Helicopters sprinkled the funeral

site with rose petals, a reminder that Nehru always wore a rose attached to his jacket. Indira sprinkled holy water over her father's body and placed a piece of sandalwood by his feet. Sanjay lit the pyre.

Indira had lost the two most important men in her life. Her sons, Rajiv and Sanjay, were away at school and offered little company. In addition, the boys were not doing well in England, which was cause for some concern. Rajiv was rapidly failing his courses at Cambridge University. He was a dismal student with little interest in studying. He met Italian Sonia Maino there and later married her. Rajiv went from Cambridge to the Rolls-Royce auto engineering school but didn't finish those studies either.

Sanjay, also never a good student, also was learning to make cars in a three-year program at Rolls-Royce. Both boys had a greater interest in engineering than in politics. Like Rajiv, Sanjay never finished the program.

After Nehru's death, India could not stand still. The Congress Party chose Lal Bahadur Shastri as prime minister. Indira was elected to Parliament, and Shastri appointed her as minister of information and broadcasting. Indira was happy enough in her Cabinet position, although she missed her father deeply.

For two years, Shastri walked in the footsteps of Nehru. On January 11, 1966, Shastri suffered a fatal heart attack. The Congress Party needed a new leader, and they turned to Indira Gandhi. ✎

6 MADAM PRIME MINISTER

꧁ꕥ꧂

When Indira Gandhi first ran for a seat in Parliament in 1964, she chose to run in her late husband's district, Rae Bareilly. This was a large district, and people knew the Gandhi name well. Feroze Gandhi was remembered fondly by local voters. Indira explained her political philosophy to her people:

> *My family is not confined to a few individuals. It consists of scores of people. Your burdens are comparatively light, because your families are limited. … But my burden is manifold [great], because scores of my family members are poverty-stricken and I have to look after them. Since they belong to different castes and creeds, they sometimes fight among themselves, and I have to intervene, especially to look after the weaker members.*

The death of the prime minister, Lal Bahadur Shastri, left a gap in the Congress Party leadership. Half a dozen candidates hoped to take his place. Each appeared qualified for the office, but there were none as able as Indira Gandhi. She spoke both English and Hindi, the two most popular languages in India. She was known throughout the world. Gandhi had no strict affiliations with a race, religion, or caste, and no known bias against any group. And she was a Nehru, a member of India's most admired family. No other candidate's qualifications matched hers.

With all of her qualifications, Indira Gandhi was the logical choice as prime minster.

The Congress Party in 1966 followed the old leadership committee, called the Syndicate. These men hoped that by choosing Gandhi, they would

have a prime minister who would follow their wishes. Indira would have the title of prime minister, but the committee would actually rule the country. They were in for a surprise. Sweet Indira had a will of iron; she was not about to be dangled in public like a puppet.

A good deal of discussion went on behind the scenes. Indira's aunt Nan Pandit supported one of Indira's opponents, Morarji Desai. Even so, she gave halfhearted backing to Indira:

> *It is a certainty that Indira Gandhi will be India's next Prime Minister. We Nehrus are very proud of our family. When a Nehru is chosen as Prime Minister, the people will rejoice. ... With a little experience she will make a fine Prime Minister. ... She is in very frail health, but with the help of her colleagues she will manage.*

Parliament's ministers gathered to vote. Gandhi received 355 out of 526 votes, with the runner-up, Morarji Desai, receiving 169. A party member announced the results. Indira Gandhi walked to the podium and spoke:

> *My heart is full, and I do not know how to thank you. ... As I stand before you my thoughts go back to the great leaders: Mahatma Gandhi, at whose feet I grew up, Panditji, my father, and Lal Bahadur Shastri. These leaders have shown the way, and I want to go along the same path.*

Prime Minister Gandhi faced a long list of problems. India had suffered a lengthy drought, bringing with it food shortages in some regions and serious famine in others. The country's economy was in dreadful condition, and inflation was making the rupee, the Indian currency, worthless. People in the northern Indian states of Nagaland and Punjab wanted to break away from India and create independent countries.

Gandhi scooped rice into a container in Calcutta to be distributed to hungry children.

Most rural Indians survived on what they grew or made themselves. When crops failed to thrive, the people suffered. Gandhi wanted to address hunger problems first. In a speech given in 1966, she said:

> *We must ensure food to our people in this year of scarcity. This is the first duty of government. We shall give urgent attention to the management and equitable distribution of food-grains, both imported and procured at home. ... Nowhere is self-reliance more urgent than in agriculture, and it means higher production, not only for meeting the domestic needs of a large and increasing population, but also for exports.*

Gandhi began an agriculture program that took advantage of scientific advances in fertilizers and seed. This program, the Green Revolution, had one goal: to feed India. With the help of science, it was hoped India would become self-sufficient in food resources.

With the economy struggling and the number of poor increasing, Gandhi realized she had to tackle inflation, which erodes the buying

American Norman Borlaug (1914–) played a major role in India's Green Revolution. Borlaug is a geneticist and botanist who developed disease-resistant, high-yield strains of wheat, rice, and other food grains. The crops grew well in India, Mexico, and other areas of the world plagued by drought or famine. For his contributions to fighting world hunger, Norman Borlaug won the Nobel Peace Prize in 1970.

power of a nation's currency. She had to get the Indian rupee under control by reducing its value compared with the money of other countries. Gandhi went on the radio to address the nation and explain why she devalued the rupee:

> *There is scarcity. The balance of payments crisis has rendered industrial capacity idle. ... Small industry has been particularly hard hit. Exports have come to a rest. Prices have moved up steeply. ... We tried various remedies. But these first-aid measures proved ineffective. Stronger medicine was necessary to restore the nation to economic health.*

Problems in the remote regions of India proved more difficult to handle. In 1967, Gandhi campaigned heavily for the Congress Party. She traveled more than 15,000 miles (24,000 km) and made 160 speeches. In Jaipur, a district dominated by the regional Swatantra Party, protests at political speeches became violent. Gandhi, standing at the microphone, was hit in the face with a stone. She suffered a swollen upper lip and a broken nose, but she did not allow the attack to stop her.

She reminded listeners that the nobles who ruled Jaipur in the past had done nothing to help them. "Go and ask the Maharajas how many wells they dug for the people in their states when they ruled them,

A huge billboard encourages Indians to vote for Gandhi's Congress Party.

how many roads they constructed, what they did to fight the slavery of the British." Gandhi continued to campaign with her nose covered in bandages.

The general election returned the Congress Party to power. However, it lost 95 seats in Parliament, leaving it with a small majority of 44 seats. The loss of seats created a rift in the Congress Party. The old leaders—the Syndicate—wanted a new leader. Gandhi insisted that she was still a good leader. She explained the party split to its members:

73

What we witness … is not a mere clash of personalities and certainly not a fight for power. It is not as simple as a conflict between the parliamentary and organizational wings. It is a conflict between two outlooks and attitudes in regard to the objectives of the Congress.

Despite efforts to keep the party together, the Congress Party split in two in 1969, with Gandhi leading the breakaway group. No sooner had she gotten past the party breakup than her youngest son involved her in a political scandal. Sanjay, who was 22 years old, applied for a license to build a small, cheap car called the Maruti. The car would cost 6,000 rupees (the equivalent of about $130 at today's exchange rates), have a maximum speed of 53 miles per hour (85 kilometers per hour), and would go a remarkable 56 miles on a gallon of gasoline.

There were 14 other bids for licenses to build cars in India. Applicants included such well-known makers as Mazda, Toyota, and Renault. Instead of an experienced carmaker, the Indian government chose Sanjay Gandhi, even though he had never produced a car. In fact, Sanjay never even finished his three-year apprenticeship with Rolls-Royce. Gandhi's political enemies shouted favoritism. And they were right. Sanjay Gandhi's company, Maruti Udyog Ltd., produced a model car that was criticized heavily, and

Indira Gandhi with her two sons, Rajiv (right) and Sanjay

in the end, Maruti Udyog never produced a single vehicle for sale.

In 1970, Sonia and Rajiv Gandhi had their first child. The boy, named Rahul, was the light of his doting grandmother's eye. She often had her three grandchildren—Rahul; his sister, Priyanka; and Sanjay and his wife Maneka's son, Varun—play in the yard while she met with her advisers or Cabinet members. At times she had her grandchildren sleep in her room at night.

Work pressures often interfered with family and personal life. Gandhi loved to read but often had to dig through a pile of government paperwork instead of enjoying a novel. She attended as many art shows and musical concerts as she could, but it was difficult to sit through a concert or opera knowing that she might be called away from the entertainment at any moment.

Family time became more precious, particularly when India found itself at war with Pakistan in 1971. Sheikh Mujibur Rahman led the East Pakistan rebellion for freedom from Pakistan. Rebels were arrested, and a reign of terror tormented the citizens. Millions of refugees poured into India to escape

Refugees from East Pakistan took shelter in concrete sewer pipes near Calcutta during the 1971 war.

the murderous Pakistani soldiers. Gandhi wanted the steady stream of refugees to end and called on Pakistan's rulers to settle with their citizens. Gandhi, and India, stood on the side of the East Pakistani people. As a result, President Agha Muhammad Yahya Khan of Pakistan ordered the bombing of Indian airfields. Suddenly, India was at war.

India quickly gained the upper hand against Pakistan. On December 16, 1971, Pakistan surrendered to combined Indian and East Pakistani forces. Indira Gandhi, often called Mother India, stood strong and firm against attacks from Pakistan. East Pakistan became the nation of Bangladesh, and today it remains a separate, independent country, thanks in part to the efforts of Indira Gandhi.

Bangladesh was once Bengali East Pakistan. The small nation is surrounded by India to the west, north, and east, and borders on Burma (Myanmar) in the southeast. It is one of the most densely populated countries in the world, and nearly 45 percent of its people live below the poverty line. Most people in Bangladesh work in farming. Two major Asian rivers run through Bangladesh— the Jamuna and the Ganges. Every year, floods pour from those rivers during the monsoon season and leave thousands homeless.

Four years later, when Gandhi proclaimed the emergency in 1975 and suspended constitutional freedom, she did so out of fear, anger, and a need to keep her position. The proclamation came from India's president and declared the existence of a grave emergency that threatened the security of India.

For two years, Indira Gandhi was India's dictator. She tried to implement a 20-point program to pull India into the 20th century. The new, modern India endured price controls on common goods. The government cut spending, while trying to build homes for the homeless. The Green Revolution continued to expand crop yields, cutting the number of famine victims. Crime was down in all areas. India thrived, but the political opposition did not think the results were worth the loss of basic freedoms. Within two years, the state of emergency came to an end, and when Indira Gandhi called for new elections, she was thrown out of office. Her greatest political enemy, the Janata Party ("people's" party in Hindi), emerged as the victor.

The leaders of the Janata Party, which was a coalition of many of the opposition parties, arranged a commission to look into Gandhi's tactics during the state of emergency. She refused to attend questioning sessions or appear before the committee. On October 3, 1977, police in an unmarked car pulled up to the Gandhi home to arrest Indira Gandhi. She asked for a bit of time to change her clothes and take care of some family business.

During the two-hour gap between the policemen's arrival and her arrest, Gandhi called friends, colleagues, and news reporters. She changed into a white sari, the color of mourning. She made a grand appearance in front of the house and in front of the cameras. That night, Gandhi went to jail, refused the food offered, and slept quite peacefully. The Janata Party's plan was to disgrace Gandhi, but it backfired. Gandhi spent one night in jail. A judge dropped the charges against her for insufficient evidence, and she came out of the ordeal more popular than ever.

She immediately set about building political support. In 1978, the Congress Party saw its second split. This time Congress (I)—for Indira—represented the forward-moving supporters of Gandhi. The other faction had a more conservative political outlook. Gandhi ran for office in Chikmagalur, a poor, rural voting district with 50 percent female voters. "Mother India" surged to the front with a 70,000-vote majority in the general election.

Within two years, Gandhi was back leading the country. She took on her second term as prime minister and truly earned the nickname Empress of India. Her son Sanjay also won a seat in the lower house of Parliament, the Lok Sabha. A few months

Indira Gandhi was very close to her son Sanjay.

later, his wife delivered a healthy son, whom they named Feroze Varun.

Life seemed ideal for Sanjay. But it all ended abruptly on June 23, 1980. Sanjay took a spin in his new Pitts S-2 A airplane, but he was not very familiar with the plane. Sanjay buzzed downward in a steep dive, a standard show-off move, but he could not pull out of it. He crashed and died instantly.

Gandhi was beside herself. Losing her father and husband had sent her into a deep depression. Losing a son was even worse. Sonia Gandhi said many years later that it seemed as though her mother-in-law "for all her courage and composure was broken in spirit."

Sanjay's funeral took place the following day. Gandhi and Maneka sat on either side of the body. Sanjay's face and body were held together by a patchwork of stitches. Rajiv, the eldest male of the family, lit the funeral pyre; within minutes, Sanjay Gandhi was reduced to ashes. ॐ

7 THE EMPRESS OF INDIA

—•—

It seemed on the surface that Indira Gandhi had led her people into the modern world. Her Green Revolution had increased food production and reduced hunger. India was fast becoming a leading force in technology. Yet not all Indians were happy with Gandhi or the Delhi government. They felt that her policies were not helping to raise the living standards of the masses.

The Sikhs, who lived in the northwestern Indian state of Punjab, believed that the government did not address their needs or recognize their rights. Much like the Southern states in the American Civil War, the Punjab wanted to separate from the rest of the nation. Violence broke out in the region, pitting Hindus and Sikhs against each other.

The Sikhs pushed to form an independent nation

Indira Gandhi greeted Indians as she campaigned throughout the country.

in Punjab called Khalistan. Gandhi said no. Government critics saw the Punjab as a blind spot in her leadership. Author and journalist Inder Malhotra said:

> *It was in Punjab ... that the real test of Indira's leadership and statesmanship lay, and it cannot be said that she withstood it with any degree of credit. On the contrary, by design, default or drift she allowed the crisis to deteriorate until the military assault on the Golden Temple became unavoidable.*

The Sikh leader Sant Jarnail Singh Bhindranwale organized a rebellion in the city of Amritsar. The rebels took over the Golden Temple and its surrounding buildings as their home base in 1982. The group had become so bold that members killed a senior police officer in daylight as he left the Golden Temple after praying. Something had to be done. By May 1984, 19 murders had taken place on the temple grounds.

Gandhi's answer was Operation Blue Star. On June 5, 1984, Indian army tanks rolled up to the Golden Temple complex. Bhindranwale was ready for his final showdown against the army. The Indian army hoped to frighten Bhindranwale and his men into surrendering. But he planned to die as a martyr and refused to negotiate a peaceful surrender.

In the first skirmishes, the Sikh rebels appeared to be winning. They popped up from underground

The Golden Temple in Amritsar is the most important Sikh holy site.

tunnels throughout the complex and fired machine guns or lobbed hand grenades at the soldiers. The army brought in tanks and began heavy fire on the building, where Bhindranwale was holed up. When he and about 50 rebels surged out of their stronghold, they met their deaths in a rain of bullets. Innocent pilgrims were also killed on the holy ground, which the Sikhs would not forget.

On October 31, 1984, Indira Gandhi prepared

Hinduism is an ancient faith with more than 880 million followers in India. Hindus believe in a universal God and several other deities. For Hindus, life is a cycle in which the individual experiences birth, death, and rebirth. Sikhism, which was founded in the 15th century, combines the traditions of Hinduism and Islam. Sikhs believe in one God and believe in the equality of all individuals. They also believe that the ideal lifestyle keeps God in the heart and mind. Most of the world's 20 million Sikhs live in the Punjab.

for a television interview with noted British actor Peter Ustinov. Throughout the summer and early fall, Gandhi had worn a bulletproof vest wherever she went and kept bodyguards close by her side. But that October day was different.

Gandhi did not wear the bulky vest because she thought it would make her look heavier on television. She dressed in a flattering saffron-colored sari and made her way along the garden path between the prime minister's home and the business office. At the gate between the two properties, Gandhi greeted an armed guard named Beant Singh.

He was a loyal Sikh who had been working in the prime minister's protection service for some time. Singh aimed his gun at Gandhi and fired into her stomach. She doubled over, blood gushing from her wounds. Another Sikh guard, Satwant Singh, appeared and emptied his submachine gun into Gandhi's bleeding body. A television crew appeared on the scene immediately. Ustinov later told *The Guardian* newspaper of London:

We were ready with the mike and the camera. A secretary had gone to fetch her, and then it happened. I heard three single shots. We looked alarmed but the people in the office said it must be firecrackers. Then there was a burst of automatic fire as if the attackers were making sure of it. I didn't think she had a chance. ... We saw soldiers running.

The two Sikh guards surrendered as other guards swarmed into the area. Later soldiers claimed that the Sikhs had tried to escape, and Beant Singh was shot and killed. Satwant Singh stood trial and in January 1986 was sentenced to death by hanging.

At the scene of the shooting, there was an ambulance, which was always kept near the prime minister's offices, but the driver and keys could not be found. Gandhi's daughter-in-law Sonia helped put Indira into a car and rushed through heavy traffic to the nearby All-India Institute of Medical Sciences. No one had alerted the emergency staff that Gandhi had been shot, so no one was prepared for her arrival. The emergency crew fell into a panic.

When Gandhi was finally taken into surgery, 80 pints of blood were pumped into her, without any hope of saving her. Doctors pronounced Indira Gandhi dead at 2:20 P.M. on October 31, 1984, although she was probably dead at the scene of the shooting. She was 66 years old. The Empress of India was gone. ॐ

8 A DYNASTY PASSED ON

꧁꧂

On the evening of his mother's assassination, Rajiv Gandhi appeared on India's government-run television station. He announced his mother's death and said:

> She was mother not only to me but to the whole nation. She served the Indian people to the last drop of her blood. The country knows with what tireless dedication she toiled for the development of India.

> You all know how dear to her heart was the dream of a united, peaceful, and prosperous India. An India in which all Indians, irrespective of their religion, language, or political persuasion, live together as one big family in an atmosphere free from mutual rivalries and prejudices.

Sonia Gandhi, president of the Congress Party, carries on the work of her mother-in-law, Indira Gandhi, and her slain husband, Rajiv.

The aftermath of Indira Gandhi's death was not peaceful, compassionate, or even rational. As Gandhi's body lay wreathed in flowers at Teen Murti House—and endless lines of mourners passed by her body, praying for her soul—violence erupted. People ran through the streets shouting, *"Khoon ka baadla khoon,"* or "Blood for blood." Many Sikhs were killed, with some estimates of the death toll ranging from 2,000 to 5,000 Sikhs.

The funeral took place on November 3, 1984, at Shantivana, a cremation site near the Jamuna River. Leaders from around the world came to honor

A group of women mourned during Indira Gandhi's funeral procession.

Indira Gandhi, including Margaret Thatcher of Great Britain, Prince Claus of the Netherlands, President Kenneth Kaunda of Zambia, and Prime Minister Nikolai Tikhonov of the Soviet Union. Secretary of State George P. Shultz represented the United States. At the funeral, mourners cried *"Indira Gandhi amar rahe"*—"Indira Gandhi will live forever."

Gandhi's body was placed on a sandalwood pyre that was doused with clarified butter. Rajiv and his son Rahul circled the body with pitchers of water. They smashed the pitchers at Indira's feet to symbolize a body's return to dust after death. Priests chanted, *"Om shanti, shanti, shanti,"* the Hindu words for "Peace be upon you." Rajiv lit the pyre, and Indira Gandhi's body was reduced to ashes.

Rajiv Gandhi, a member of Parliament, was tapped to be India's next prime minister. His family—wife Sonia, daughter Priyanka, and son Rahul—now stood in the political spotlight. Rajiv may have had a family history of political greatness, but that greatness did not pass down to him. He had no interest in helping India's poor and watched helplessly as inflation reached nearly 10 percent. Government spending ran wild, as did the national debt. During Rajiv's term in office, national debt expanded from $23 billion to $35 billion.

As the poor became even poorer, Rajiv's friends became richer at the people's expense. Scandals and corruption exploded. One such scandal occurred

Prime Minister Rajiv Gandhi and his wife, Sonia (wearing glasses), met with supporters in local dress.

when India bought guns from the Swedish firm Bofors. The contract was arranged through Gandhi's friends, and they received kickbacks, or large commissions, for their efforts. After five years of Rajiv Gandhi's leadership, people had had enough. After the 1989 general election, Rajiv kept his seat in Parliament, but his party held only 197 of 545 seats in the Lok Sabha. Congress (I) lost the prime minister's position.

In 1991, Rajiv put forth an extra effort to regain power. While he was campaigning, he was assassinated by a bomb as he made a speech in southern India. Indira Gandhi's immediate family was now dead.

As the 20th century came to a close, the British Broadcasting Corporation in England asked its viewers and listeners to vote for the most influential woman in the past 1,000 years. Indira Gandhi came in first. Few men or women have left such a valued mark on their country or on the world.

Indira Gandhi sacrificed her personal life in support of a new, blossoming nation. She was quiet and private. As a young woman, she hated making speeches, but her life's work demanded she give up her retiring nature and speak out. Perhaps she loved her husband too little, but, without doubt, she loved her children too much. She indulged them and failed to teach them the same values of hard work and patriotism that she learned at her father's knee.

Politically, Indira Gandhi believed that all people could live together, without regard to race, religion,

After Rajiv Gandhi's assassination, his wife, Sonia, Italian by birth and Indian by marriage, eventually turned to politics and is currently a leader in the Congress Party. She joined the party in 1997 and rose to party president in 1998. On May 28, 2005, Sonia Gandhi was elected president of the Indian National Congress in a landslide victory. This made her the fifth member of the Nehru clan to lead India's Congress. The others were Motilal Nehru, Jawaharlal Nehru, Indira Gandhi, and Rajiv Gandhi.

or heritage. She professed belief in the ideal of democracy but assumed dictatorial powers and suspended constitutional liberties. She thrust India's successes and concerns into the world spotlight while she pushed her country toward a socialist economy. She attempted to concentrate more and more power in her own hands, with mixed results. She achieved great advances for India in technology, education, and world affairs, but while many felt she was a great success, others considered her a failure. Sudheendra Kulkarni, an Indian writer and editor, said of Gandhi:

Indira Gandhi dedicated her life to India, her beloved country.

I can neither fully condemn nor fully praise [her]. ... She killed the spirit of dissent and democracy in the Congress Party. And since that party also happens to be the largest, oldest, and, in many ways, the only national political organization in the country, the erosion of democracy in the Congress also meant grievous injury to the democratic process in India as a whole.

Some critics saw Indira Gandhi as political from head to toe. She knew how to hold power and how to wield it. During her life, people called her the Iron Lady of India, Mother India, and the Empress of India. Few world leaders have had her determination and drive, her compassion for her people, or her dedication to her country. As Rajiv Gandhi said on the night his mother died, "Indira Gandhi is no more, but her soul lives. India lives. India is immortal."

GANDHI'S LIFE

1942

Marries Feroze
Gandhi

1917

Born November 19 in
Allahabad, India

1936

Mother, Kamala
Kaul Nehru, dies in
Switzerland

1940

1917

Vladimir Lenin and
Leon Trotsky lead
Bolsheviks in a
rebellion against the
Russian government
during the October
Revolution

1936

African-American
athlete Jesse Owens
wins four gold medals
at the Olympic Games
in Berlin in the
face of Nazi racial
discrimination

1942

Japanese Americans
are placed in intern-
ment camps because
of fear of disloyalty
during World War II
(1939–1945)

WORLD EVENTS

1942–1943

Serves time in Naini prison, as does her husband

1944

Son Rajiv is born

1946

Son Sanjay is born

1945

1943

U.S. General Dwight D. Eisenhower becomes the supreme Allied commander

1944

Operation Overlord begins on D-Day with the landing of 155,000 Allied troops on the beaches of Normandy, France; it is the largest amphibious military operation in history

1946

Nazi war criminals are executed after trials in Nuremberg, Germany

GANDHI'S LIFE

1959

Becomes
president of the
Congress Party

1948

Mohandas Gandhi is
killed by an assassin

1947

Father, Jawaharlal
Nehru, is prime
minister and Indira
serves as first lady
when India becomes
an independent nation

1959

Fidel Castro becomes
leader of Cuba

1948

The modern nation of
Israel is founded

WORLD EVENTS

1960

Husband dies of
a heart attack

1964

Father dies while in
office; Indira elected
to Parliament

1966–1977

Serves as prime
minister

1965

1961

Soviet cosmonaut Yuri
Gagarin is the first
human to enter space

1966

The National
Organization for
Women (NOW) is
established to work
for equality between
women and men

GANDHI'S LIFE

1975

Takes over the country under the Emergency Order Proclamation

1977

Ousted as prime minister by the Janata Party; goes to jail for one day

1978

Runs for a new seat in Parliament

1975

1978

The first test-tube baby conceived outside its mother's womb is born in Oldham, England

1975

Bill Gates and Paul Allen found Microsoft, which will become the world's largest software company

WORLD EVENTS

1980

Becomes prime minister again; son Sanjay dies in an airplane crash

1982

Sikh rebels take over the Golden Temple in Amritsar; Operation Blue Star launched in 1984

1984

Assassinated on October 31 by her Sikh bodyguards

1980

1980

The United States boycotts the Olympic Games in Moscow in protest of the Soviet invasion of Afghanistan

1981

IBM introduces the first personal computer

1984

U.S. scientists isolate the virus that causes AIDS (acquired immune deficiency syndrome), which will become a worldwide epidemic

DATE OF BIRTH: November 19, 1917

PLACE OF BIRTH: Allahabad, India

FATHER: Jawaharlal Nehru
(1889–1964)

MOTHER: Kamala Kaul Nehru
(1899–1936)

EDUCATION: Badminton School,
Bristol, England;
Oxford University

SPOUSE: Feroze Gandhi
(1913–1960)

DATE OF MARRIAGE: March 26, 1942

CHILDREN: Rajiv (1944–1991)
Sanjay (1946–1980)

DATE OF DEATH: October 31, 1984

**PLACE OF
CREMATION:** Delhi, India

FURTHER READING

Dommermuth-Costa, Carol. *Indira Gandhi: Daughter of India.* Minneapolis: Lerner Publications, 2002.

Ganeri, Anita. *Indira Gandhi.* Chicago: Heinemann Library, 2003.

Rowe, Percy, and Patience Coster. *Delhi.* Milwaukee: World Almanac Library, 2005.

Roy, Anita. *India.* Chicago: Raintree, 2006.

Shores, Lori. *Teens in India.* Minneapolis: Compass Point Books, 2007.

LOOK FOR MORE SIGNATURE LIVES BOOKS ABOUT THIS ERA:

Benazir Bhutto: *Pakistani Prime Minister and Activist*

Fidel Castro: *Leader of Communist Cuba*

Madame Chiang Kai-shek: *Face of Modern China*

Winston Churchill: *British Soldier, Writer, Statesman*

Jane Goodall: *Legendary Primatologist*

Adolf Hitler: *Dictator of Nazi Germany*

Benito Mussolini: *Italian Dictator*

Queen Noor: *American-born Queen of Jordan*

Eva Perón: *First Lady of Argentina*

Joseph Stalin: *Dictator of the Soviet Union*

ON THE WEB

For more information on this topic, use FactHound.

1. Go to *www.facthound.com*
2. Type in this book ID: 0756518857
3. Click on the *Fetch It* button.

FactHound will find the best Web sites for you.

HISTORIC SITES

Asian Art Museum
200 Larkin St.
San Francisco, CA 94102
415/581-3500
Exhibits include a collection of Indian sculpture, paintings, and carvings and the only gallery in the Western Hemisphere devoted to Sikh art

Mahatma Gandhi Memorial
Across from the Indian Embassy
near Dupont Circle
Washington, DC
202/939-7000
A monument dedicated to the man who encouraged nonviolent resistance in India's struggle for freedom

apartheid
a former policy of racial segregation and discrimination in South Africa

boycott
to refuse to do business with someone as a form of protest

communism
system in which goods and property are owned by the government and shared in common

cremation
the act of reducing a body to ashes by burning

dictator
ruler who takes complete control of a country, often unjustly

exploitation
the act of using something in an unfair or unjust way for selfish reasons

gurudwaras
Sikh places of worship

sanatorium
an institution for rest and maintaining or improving health

socialism
an economic system in which the government owns most businesses

Vedic
relating to the Vedas, a Hindu collection of hymns, prayers, and other sacred writings

Zoroastrian
followers of one of the world's oldest religions, considered the first whose followers believe in one God

Chapter 1

Page 9, line 8: Inder Malhotra. *Indira Gandhi: A Personal and Political Biography.* London: Hodder & Stoughton, 1989, p. 163.

Page 13, line 3: Katherine Frank. *Indira: The Life of Indira Nehru Gandhi.* Boston: Houghton Mifflin Company, 2002, p. 374.

Page 13, line 22: Ibid., p. 377.

Page 14, line 21: Tariq Ali. *An Indian Dynasty.* New York: G. P. Putnam's Sons, 1985, p. 146.

Page 14, line 26: *Indira: The Life of Indira Nehru Gandhi*, p. 381.

Chapter 2

Page 19, line 10: Pranay Gupte. *Mother India: A Political Biography of Indira Gandhi.* New York: Charles Scribner's Sons, 1992, p. 136.

Page 20, line 4: *Indira Gandhi: A Personal and Political Biography*, p. 26.

Page 22, line 8: *Indira Gandhi Quotes.* The Quotations Page. 20 Oct. 2006. www.quotationspage.com/quotes/Indira_Gandhi/

Page 22, line 22: *Mother India: A Political Biography of Indira Gandhi*, p. 135.

Page 25, line 3: *Indira Gandhi: A Personal and Political Biography*, p. 34.

Page 26, line 17: Ibid., p. 36.

Page 28, line 2: *Mother India: A Political Biography of Indira Gandhi*, p. 152.

Page 28, line 17: Ibid., p. 153.

Chapter 3

Page 35, line 10: Ibid., p. 187.

Page 36, line 3: *Indira Gandhi: A Personal and Political Biography*, p. 43.

Page 37, line 23: Ibid., p. 48.

Page 38, line 3: Indira Gandhi. *My Truth.* New York: Grove Press, Inc., 1980, p. 50.

Page 39, line 11: *Mother India: A Political Biography of Indira Gandhi*, p. 195.

Page 39, line 19: Ibid.

Page 41, line 11: Ibid., p. 199.

Chapter 4

Page 45, line 9: *My Truth*, pp. 50–51.

Page 46, line 17: Ibid., p. 52.

Page 47, line 14: Ibid., p. 53.

Page 48, line 2: *Mother India: A Political Biography of Indira Gandhi*, p. 211.

Page 49, line 12: *My Truth*, p. 55.

Page 51, line 1: Pupul Jayakar. *Indira Gandhi: An Intimate Biography*. New York: Random House, Inc., 1992, p.100.

Page 51, line 9: *My Truth*, p. 58.

Page 53, line 5: *Muslim Population Figures by Country*. Invest East. 24 July 2006. www.factbook.net/muslim_pop.php

Page 53, line 20: Indira Gandhi. *Indira Gandhi: Speeches & Writings*. New York: Harper & Row, 1975, p. 25.

Page 54, line 8: Ibid., p. 37.

Chapter 5

Page 60, line 4: *Indira Gandhi: An Intimate Biography*, p. 113.

Page 60, line 19: *Mother India: A Political Biography of Indira Gandhi*, p. 249.

Page 61, line 19: Ibid., p. 232.

Page 62, line 11: *Indira: The Life of Indira Nehru Gandhi*, p. 258.

Page 62, line 24: *Indira Gandhi: An Intimate Biography*, pp. 115-116.

Page 63, line 25: *Mother India: A Political Biography of Indira Gandhi*, p. 257.

Page 64, line 7: Ibid., p. 258.

Chapter 6

Page 67, line 7: *An Indian Dynasty*, p. 161.

Page 69, line 10: *Indira: The Life of Indira Nehru Gandhi*, p. 291.

Page 69, line 23: Ibid., p. 292.

Page 71, line 5: Indira Gandhi. *Peoples and Problems*. London: Hodder and Stoughton, 1982, p. 10.

Page 72, line 6: *Indira: The Life of Indira Nehru Gandhi*, p. 298.

Page 72, line 27: *An Indian Dynasty*, p. 160.

Page 74, line 1: *Indira: The Life of Indira Nehru Gandhi*, p. 317.

Page 81, line 12: Ibid., p. 448.

Chapter 7

Page 84, line 4: *Indira Gandhi: A Personal and Political Biography*, p. 287.

Page 87, line 1: Ibid., p. 17.

Chapter 8

Page 89, line 4: *Mother India: A Political Biography of Indira Gandhi*, p. 81.

Page 95, line 1: Ibid., p. 113.

Page 95, line 18: Ibid., p. 81.

Ali, Tariq. *An Indian Dynasty*. New York: G.P. Putnam's Sons, 1985.

Bhatia, Krishan. *Indira*. New York: Praeger, 1974.

Frank, Katherine. *Indira: The Life of Indira Nehru Gandhi*. Boston: Houghton Mifflin Company, 2002.

Gandhi, Indira. *Indira Gandhi: Speeches & Writings*. New York: Harper & Row, 1975.

Gandhi, Indira. *My Truth*. New York: Grove Press, Inc., 1980.

Gandhi, Indira. *Peoples and Problems*. London: Hodder and Stoughton, 1982.

Gupte, Pranay. *Mother India: A Political Biography of Indira Gandhi*. New York: Charles Scribner's Sons, 1992.

Jayakar, Pupul. *Indira Gandhi: An Intimate Biography*. New York: Random House, Inc., 1992.

Malhotra, Inder. *Indira Gandhi: A Personal and Political Biography*. London: Hodder & Stoughton, 1989.

Barbara A. Somervill has been writing for more than 30 years. She has written newspaper and magazine articles, video scripts, and books for children. She enjoys writing about history and science and investigating people's lives for biographies. Ms. Somervill lives with her husband in South Carolina.

Image Credits